LOVE'S LAST NUMBER

ALSO BY CHRISTOPHER HOWELL

The Crime of Luck

Why Shouldn't I

Though Silence: The Ling Wei Texts

Sea Change

Sweet Afton

Memory and Heaven

Just Waking

Light's Ladder

Dreamless and Possible: Poems New and Selected

Gaze

LIMITED EDITIONS

The Bear in the Mirror

The Jetty

Red Alders in an Island Dream

The Wu General Writes from Far Away

Lady of the Fallen Air (from the Chinese)

King of the Butterflies

ANTHOLOGY

Aspects of Robinson: Homage to Weldon Kees

(with Christopher Buckley)

LOVE'S
LAST
NUMBER

POEMS

CHRISTOPHER HOWELL

milkweed
editions

Published 2017 by Milkweed Editions
Printed in the United States of America
Cover design by Ryan Scheife / Mayfly Design
Cover illustration by Adam Hall
Author photo by Joni Sternbach
17 18 19 20 21   5 4 3 2 1
First Edition

Milkweed Editions, an independent nonprofit publisher, gratefully acknowledges sustaining support from the Jerome Foundation; the Lindquist & Vennum Foundation; the McKnight Foundation; the National Endowment for the Arts; the Target Foundation; and other generous contributions from foundations, corporations, and individuals. Also, this activity is made possible by the voters of Minnesota through a Minnesota State Arts Board Operating Support grant, thanks to a legislative appropriation from the arts and cultural heritage fund, and a grant from the Wells Fargo Foundation. For a full listing of Milkweed Editions supporters, please visit www.milkweed.org.

Library of Congress Cataloging-in-Publication Data
Names: Howell, Christopher, author.
Title: Love's last number : poems / Christopher Howell.
Description: Minneapolis : Milkweed Editions, 2017.
Identifiers: LCCN 2016029439| ISBN 9781571314758 (softcover : acid-free paper) | ISBN 9781571319333 (ebook)
Classification: LCC PS3558.O897 A6 2017 | DDC 811/.54—dc23
LC record available at https://lccn.loc.gov/2016029439

For Jim Johnsrud, David Luckert,
Richard Morgan & Carlos Reyes

CONTENTS

1. THE AGNOSTIC PIROUETTES

2. THE WRONG ANGELS

3. THE UNATTAINABLE NOW

1.

THE AGNOSTIC PIROUETTES

Do you know, Daphne, that song of the old days,
At the foot of the sycamore or under the white laurels,
Under the olive trees, the myrtle, or the trembling willows,
That song of love that always begins again?

—Robert Duncan

A SHORT SONG

This is a song of our consciousness, that faltering
old man who will never make it across the bridge,
who sits down in the grit and dust of it with his wrinkled sack
of groceries that will have to last. A song of his foolish bravery
and terror, his hope that will not stay focused, that wanders
a springtime path between peach trees
and the berries, humming something, forgetting,
and humming again. A song of his wishes
tossing their hats in the wind and watching the last boat
depart, its cargo of nameless meaning casting flowers, waving
out of sight as the sun goes down.
It is a song of memory's little ways and sudden corner-like loveliness
turned to smoke and broken glass it eats and eats
to stay marginally alive. A song of the bridge that never ends
really, and never whispers this
as the old man listens for the one spot of silence
or the one clear voice that might be his.

DESPERATELY COMPOSED

I wake on a small raft
and see her swimming away
with a cat under each arm
and wearing the sun
like a kind of sombrero.
Again I have not been chosen.
What will I drink, so far from land?
Where will I find flowers enough
to keep me breathing what
St. Francis called "the Perfect Air,"
the pneuma of hope's tiny bells
announcing the hours of supplication
and grace?

She is far from me now, a speck
rising and dipping on the dazzle,
on a glinting of green trumpets that call
and call as Mahler drifts past

in a clef-shaped canoe and I toss him
a story in which a man dreams himself
beyond thought, beyond the farthest
point of land, where what he loves
has left him widened and cloudy,
the great sky somehow come
into his broken-fingered notation
turning slowly all night, lifting
as I do, waving to her, imploring

the angels to open themselves,
tune their instruments and pretend
that he is one of them, or they
more of him than he can count.

CROSSING JORDAN

Having eaten the chickens, dogs, cattle, horses, our belts,
leather vests, and shoes, we came at last to the river,
great silver-blue spillage carving its monument and grave
in the endless grass.

We fell face down and drank, a writhing stillness
filling us like lust
or the sort of prayer they don't
teach you.

Leaves revolved on the stream like golden boats, carelessly adrift,
open to the sky that seemed to be watching as we herded small fish
into the shallows and ate them alive
and squirming.

Later we made fire in the shadow of a cutbank
and slept and rose and ate and drank again and slept
and on the third day
we rose

as our Lord, to whom we had prayed all the way from St. Joe
and who had indeed delivered us
so that we thought the far shore surely must flow with milk
and something sweet.

So we made our crossing, the stream being wide but shallow.
Only one nine-year-old boy broke the human chain and so
was swept away.

Brother Jacoby said it was what God and the river required
by way of sacrifice, and the boy's father went for him with a knife.
Thus discord came upon us and a taint
upon the new land

so that some of us longed for our lives as they had been
before we dared to cross the glinting vein, before
we dared the Lord to give us
everything.

But, finally, with the river at our backs it seemed wrong
to think of this.
Praise the Lord and his angels, we said, when we buried the torn
and bloated boy,

who had reached down with both hands for something bright
in the water.

BUT BEFORE THAT

we lay awake all night, dreams thickening
like hair in the cold branches
and ready to descend, ready to know
what had become and what would be.
She said, "I thought just now an owl
flew out of me, an emerald being, a species
of moon."
And I said, "Sometimes."

It was so cold we grew afraid of a warmth
that moved in the woods nearby, beginning
to curl toward us like a smile.
So we prayed and the sun came up with not
a single barnyard crowing, not one worried dog.

We ate snow and kissed and thought of dancing.
We knew where we were and that we were
what others would call an escape ecstatic
with grief because we were so few,
because our shadows wore so many
unforgettable strangers.

So there would be warmth and food, and still days
by the river. There would be each other again
and again in the light of a naked
and forgiving room. There would be nameless
secrets that would need nothing but to ask
"Does anyone really survive?"
and keep on asking.

CONNECTIVITY

A huge ball of twine turns to bread
and feeds the five thousand, Jesus unrolling it
and watching the sky for signs.

In the church on the hill someone has lost

the thread
of her devotion while underground
the minotaur sings sadly of a boy
strung out, lost in the maze
of shopping carts and limited offers
and girls undressed, the gold filigree
of youth lying

all about them, worshippers
filing past whatever follows something thin
and pale, amazed, loaves and fishes

and twine if you have it.

Let those who hunger stretch forth
their hands, all right?

Let something come to show
whose world [is this?]
and which thread is more miraculous
than dust.

Bright red. Blue. Something heavy
near your heart as Christ stands
on the hillside of empty baskets, fish-bone trash
and crusts of rye, immense cat's cradle
above him in the sky.

DIMINISHING RETURNS

A crow sits in the dark, thinking
I'm an owl scouring this field for mice.

Then he thinks, I'm suddenly wise, too:
rem acu tetigisti, brother.

He looks in all his leafy cupboards
for testimonials and diplomas.

Finding none, he says, perhaps
I am an hawk, and he can feel

his beak bend down and a pleasurable
bloodlust fill his mind like gasoline.

Oh, I'm a killer now, I am,
he says to his glinting talons,

but it's night, I really ought to be
sleeping. So he sleeps. In his dream

he is a melon and a huge blade
severs one half of him from the other.

When he wakes, falling, he is two
blackbirds with one wing each.

THE BODY IN MOTION

Is it true that things return
when they are not the same,
that they wait
till recognition bends
like water around a rock
and we say, oh, it is almost you
whom I touched in the blades
of forest light
naked as you were and have been
always in that room in me where you live
like clear water in a bowl.
And you *are* not the same, yet
here you are. Clearly the beautiful
spirit clothed in time
persists
and I bow to that, smoothing
its bright leaves and surrender,
its wanting to be known.

KANSAS

A man is standing in a field
at the edge of a town so small
it sometimes forgets itself and goes home
to its pale, lopsided houses and dry, leaf-filled
fishponds in the weedy corners
of its yards. If it's almost dark
someone might suppose
he has come to lift his arms and ask
for a life that would remember him
or for a vision of horses wading toward the moon
just rising to signal that all's well. But
as to that, who knows; so far

it might as well mean his mother

is calling her old dog in
from the barn, the barn that burned
and the dog that has been dead for fifty years.
He might as well be anyone come to that edge
that says things end
at the beginning of something else, that even wind
fingering the grass
knows this, teasing his mother's mad white hair
in another life, where the fields continue to begin,
where the path that brought him ends and doesn't care
how large or far or bright the rising moon, or if the dog
comes a last time when she calls.

THIS MORTAL COIL

1. On the Nature of Things

Lucretius believed that contentment could not be
contained, since soul is its definitive essence,

and since the particular shade of its formality
insists soul be experienced as a long, empty

stretch of beach. Evening reminds me of this.
Windows brighten with darkness and lilac leaves

brush their shadows into place. The daylilies fall
to their knees. One by one the moments become

themselves as Lucretius, in a golf shirt and slacks,
examines their unassuming surprise. He is not

surprised, on this street of bungalows and modest
swank. From one of the interstices between worlds,

he looks back at the future that's eyeing him
and scratches under his left arm. In a while he will

join me on my porch. Four hundred miles inland,
we will contemplate the sea and he will remind me

again that death is nothing to us.

2. The After Hours Afterlife

The drummer sets down his tools
and the lights come up.
Four men hop in circles to describe their joy.
The hostess is secretly aflame with a grapelike fullness
I can't bear to watch. Perhaps the sky is not, as we have been told,
the province of gods, but of spaniels.
I think of Henry Ford and the Pyramid Society
as the drummer lights a foot-long cigarette and places his wig on
a stand.
Tolstoy is the barman and refuses all payment
in the name of virtue.
Usual women slide between the chairs.
When someone shouts "Fire," everyone laughs
but Tolstoy
who is busy pouring crème de menthe into a whiskey bottle
as I tell him I'm a big fan, that I've read *Crime and Peace* six times.
He says, "The butler did it,
or the drummer." He hasn't decided.
The four men are now hopping in squares
and their barking falls like a dark blue snow of sound.
The cigarette girl wants to have the drummer's baby.
Tolstoy hands me money and a horrible drink
and says, "I died in a train station. I'll bet you didn't know that."
Then he throws back his head and screams, "Last call!
All aboard!"

3. The Parable as Originally Told

It was a story nobody knew,
a nobody-could-possibly-know-it story
more or less untold: a man with no arms
finds a railroad spike and a hunk of cheese
beside a dying cat. To the man
with no arms the cat says, "When I must shed
this mortal coil, this veil of fleas, it is my fondest
wish that these my only possessions
should pass to someone worthy of their panic
lustre, their *duende*. Are you such a one, oh man
with no arms?"
The man with no arms enters a frenzy of nodding
and falls forward upon these treasures, devouring
the spike straight away
and peering curiously at the cheese.

The End

4. *I'm Not Sure about Dying*

on a day like this one, low clouds
with some rain in them
and some Mendelssohn tuning a broken viola
for a child
and the one-legged waiter at McLeary's
whistling like a god full of birds.
I'm not sure I want to go off
on a breeze such as this that strokes the awning
above a battered door, with the portrait of Jean-Paul Sartre
carved just under the top hinge next to the sign
that reminds you to abandon all hope
every time it opens, and reads "Just kidding" when it shuts.
On such a day I'm not sure
what my hands mean by what they can't contain, that blue
shimmer years ago above the white
and my father's voice from far down beyond
the chicken coop where bees liked to sip the little daisies
and our old dog slept all afternoon. In spite of the distance
I turn toward that window in Kansas with the beautiful quietude
inside it and ask my hands to pray for me again
that I *not* die on such a day
that the rope bridge hold for one more crossing
that my shoes understand their mission
that the hunchback and broken boy float free of pain
that none of us turn to glass before our time.

5. Edward Hopper

Red dress, hat like a cake
beaten flat by hammers,
she stands against the wall, one hip cocked, lip
curled up at a corner, and in her eye
a passionate antipondering upon revenge.
Did her father come at her
with a drill? Did her brothers hold her down
and look? Ask someone who talks to God.
If you really want to know, there's a nickel
plated .32 in her lamé bag
and the creamy edge of a hundred-dollar bill

broods from her black left shoe
like a signal or a dare. And what could the signal say?
I want you? Leave me alone
because the wall behind me glows?

A man in boots says, "Hey, baby, dance?"
But no, she wants a bourbon
and Coke, a new start, slippery skin
and something snappy for a name.
She wants the sea's green zero and a hen-like calm.
She'd like to know if she exists and how much
existing might cost. A hundred more or less
be enough? She wonders
what it's like being dead, if being
dead means you're free; you kick off
your shoes and then you dance.

ASTRONOMY LESSON

I had dreamed all day of baseball
and a girl named Darlene
and therefore stood at the blackboard
like a blind conductor imagining the orchestra
as a field it would take years to cross.
The teacher loomed over me, gloating,
disgusted, had-it-up-to-here in her blue
cotton dress with its belt of little mother-of-pearl
moons I wanted to touch. Near the school day's end
she had suddenly, it seemed to me, shouted, "Christopher!
Which planet in our solar system is closest to Earth?"
Who could know, I thought, who could know
even what it *meant* to know
when you could call it anything you liked
and, looking out the window,
could *imagine* yourself there—and be back
before the end of class, or the end predicted
every weekday by that man with the sign who wept
as he ran down Hawthorn Street,
begging us all to repent.

And, of course, I wanted to repent
of my lazy and ignorant life, its obvious
worthlessness to anyone but my mother
who saw nothing wrong and who would be puzzled
again at my having to stay after school confused
and humiliated at the blackboard

writing "Dreaming makes one stupid" over and over, slowly,
the teacher with her arms crossed, tapping a foot.
If *only* I would pay attention!
What
would become of me?
She was sure she didn't know.

Above us the new moon went by
and all the daylight stars
telling their stories without a sound, though
the man with the sign was listening hard
to his own numb heart
and, at the blackboard, I fixed on the white curve
of the letter S, in "stupid," like a pathway I could follow
out of the den of that gorgon
who knew everything except the sun's certain anger
at her wearing moons
around her waist like that, as though she herself
were a planet
where no one would ever repent
and children were despised.

SAVING FACE

Children were catching faces in dip nets.
Sometimes they caught the moon and set it
adrift again.
High in the trees great birds kept screeching,
"Wrong! Wrong! This lamp should be bigger,
more severe!"

But the children went on angling
for faces, always
those of strangers, staring and surprised
at their detachment, lifted and fluttering
like moths above a pond.
In the pale blue shallows nearby, the less visible

faces of sleepers bumped delicately, dreaming
of glass bones. Later a bus
of fog and light collected these
and drove off toward the edge of town
where suffering woke and took them
home to their sadly childlike bodies.

TINY BEES CLUNG TO US

like hats in a high wind, though
there was no wind and the border
lay only a mile or two ahead.
Cross it and be free, we thought,
holding each other a last time
before dashing out, heedless of patrols
scouring the hills for we who were hated,
we who believed.
And because of our belief, perhaps, the bees

were soft and stingless
all through that day, warming us, whispering
of secret ways, humming a tune we followed

like a path.
And later, what a night it was! Loving
in a roofless ruin, starlight
falling over us like music we had never heard,
like joy's lanterns, diamond bees
spending themselves as we were spent, lighting up
the dark hives over which we knew God
bent as though happy
or blind.

OUT OF SEQUENCE

Quarks and quasars and white dwarves
notwithstanding, the night display
through snow-lined traceries of the sycamores
has been watching us
a long time, slowly shaking
its beglittered head.

*

This morning in snow under the eaves,
squirrel tracks
then, a little way on, cat tracks, the strides
lengthening out toward a confusion of bloody snow
less than two feet from the immense elm:

tough luck.

*

In my sleep I am rowing away from summer
as though it were an island
or a clump of trees.
Fall is up ahead, I can feel the bright leaves
and smoky quiet of the air.
My cat is with me in the boat and has eyes
only for the twinkling flights of starlings, synchronized,
angular and fluid, over the green embankment
and the water.

Downstream winter's fingers flex and glint.
The cat is indifferent to fear, but I perceive
the truth: this boat will not be anchored or
turned back. More tough luck.

*

If there weren't so many stars,
if squirrels died quietly, if cats were vegetarian,
if I were not welded to the deck
of this boat with only one port of call,
I would show you the angelic presences
who never die.
I could fuse frayed lines of drift and clasp them
to me as the journey found its names.
Out of my hollowness and fasting,
out of the great winter trees, I would complete myself
inside of time
with whatever walks there and whatever universe
came calling.

*

The boat turns like bones in a dream of the dragon's
transformation, grey to yellow to grey,
scales or lights centripetally shed
as current's essential mystery grips itself.
In the prow Socrates questions the politicians.
In the stern St. Joan is up in smoke.
Amidships where my cat and I peer in slantwise

amazement, Jesus is counting something
and handing bits of it into the sky, saying, "Take, eat,
who knows when we shall find ourselves again
so blessedly alive?"

TWO POEMS IN WHICH HE THINKS OF HER

I.

Someone, he thought, may be wading
in a blue-scarf afternoon, a coastal
poppy-littered zone where one breath
and the next may be
nearly enough. This thought
in the room of a single step
made him shiver. What was the use
of moments, if not this
near dream, someone's face congealing
like three crows suddenly one
thing
in an orange tree.

His hands admired themselves
as he walked, as though certain of a train's
arrival or a boat safe at sea.
His hair almost white, he thought
of someone beautiful beside him, some kind
of rose delirium of which the crows
would take no notice. He thought of
the swing and simple logic
of her movement, her cloudy light.
He thought, "This is my thought,"
and turned away
from what he thought.

II.

He was astonished by her face
with its aura of blonde amazement
behind dark glass, impressionist
and fleeting.
It may have been prayer
brought her, or the single shaft
of sun knifing out of a disaster
to illuminate a pot of daisies
beside the walk.
Hers was the momentary face
on a train passing, whispering the blue
of Kandinsky's horses, a half moon
lost in the hills no one knew
were there. Hers was the face rain paints
on glass and seen by accident
having looked up, vaguely troubled.

THE PRINCIPAL UNCERTAINTY

The beautiful women complain about their men
whose souls are bent by blindnesses and rage,
whose hearts freeze in the rain of all they realize
they cannot be.
The beautiful women rise, and kick
and spin, nuzzling their sorrows
like small dogs or children they have found
sleeping behind the A&P
as the moon lunges past, surly and dimmed
by clouds, broken like ancient money.
And don't come back! the women holler to their men.
And don't leave, either! And for Godsake save yourself
and the children! Then they look up,
fixing the moon in place, just as Heisenberg said was possible only
outside of time.

Oh we love love
love the moon, the women croon
sadly
to themselves.
And the café doors close and the lights
go out.

*

On the long walk back to his torn house,
Death
remembers the beautiful women, a certain half-lit angle

of the face and then the fall and swing of shining
tresses, cream of the neckline's
descent.
And suddenly Death wishes they would never
be his, that they would keep themselves or the moon
take all their blood into itself
and let him sleep.

*

But is it true
love is a stranger
or a stone? something asks
as the silent men sit beside the fire
that is always among them. Every so often
one of them, heavy with wordlessness, rises
and throws himself into the flames.

*

Is there elegy enough for this: women
and beauty and men and death
and the moon?
God's loneliness enters it
all, like the night air after a storm
when there is nothing to do but breathe
and listen
for the voices of those who survived.

AN AS-THOUGH PRAYER

As though nothing mattered I pray
for an indefinable relief, a tree
for instance, out of the arms
of which anything might step
restored; or a blue boat waiting
at the margin of a pond no one
has seen for three hundred years.
I pray for angels and all things
that cannot exist,
that they enter the room
behind me and still be there
when I turn—even their likenesses
will do. I pray for the ache
that keeps me and the staircase
of that keeping. I pray for the soft
recumbence of moss, that memory
not desert this. I pray for the violin
I imagine in an attic on the edge
of a broken Kansas town
where wind scours the paintless
barns leaning and empty in the fields,
that it be found by a child, all angular
softness and hands atremble.
I pray for the lamplit bus stop
and the sour green apple left
beside a book in the shadow
of my left arm thirty years ago.
I pray for my daughter

under the grass. I put my head
in my hands. I pray for my hands
and the work thereof.
I pray for my soul though it may
not matter, though the line
is dead and the sky within me
falling, dark, and starless, a huge
crow contending there with God's
emptiness or God's hopeful
and faraway gleam.

2.

THE WRONG ANGELS

Érxias, where is all this useless army gathering to go?

—ARCHILOCHUS

VILLAGE

Before the war
what did we know? The clouds
were great ships and small
scudding the blue calm.
When I walked to the corner
others were there, moving
parts of a stillness.
Grey old men dozed on benches
checkered with yellow leaves.
"Pass the butter," one of them
would murmur, or,
"Tell me the one I used to like."
Before the war every day
was the more or less happy stranger
going his ways.
The ragman knocked at my door
and the goat girl
waved to show me her clean hands.
Some of us thought of the Christ
and some of the white wood
stacked and clean smelling
by the sheds.
Whole days went by without
a single prayer cringing
like a refugee under a bridge.
The sun came up and down, dreadless
light wheeling from its hair.
Before the war longing had shoes

and dust from which to turn away.
I washed and slept and rose
and washed and slept.
Most of what was lost came home
changed, muttering
that beyond the river something wrong
was on the way.

TIN SOLDIERS

I.

They lined up
to execute the prisoner
dragged like a collapsed tent
from the cell he kept insisting was home.

II.

I didn't know what waited
or went. I stood
beneath her window in the rain,
my prayers cold as clouds,

the drenched butterfly of my hope
wandering in circles,
my enemy shining like brass
in an ocean of red hair and pigs.

III.

Furnace of roses, river of mirrored
evenings, my secret gates were nothing, less
than a name on a stone.
The squadsmen lifted their guns.

I SAID TO GOD, "I'M THINKING OF YOU"

Nevertheless, the rain continued.
In dark doorways and under loading docks
men slept with cardboard and cold.

I said, "My heart is full with praising
your justice." Still, the sniper drew in
a long terrible breath—or so I understand.

I said I was lonely for my old body
and my body became older still.
I said suffering had become too friendly

among us and that everyone had begun
to look like everyone else.
I said the various prophets were not much

listened to and that He should try some
other tack, that I had malign fears.
I said consequence was immeasurable.

I said, "Dear God, if you remember me,
remember us."

THE WRONG ANGELS

1. *Edvard Munch*

She came down the road
like a piece of the road dissevered
from itself by two legs and a shoe.
She carried a rat trap basket of brown
and brittle flowers: her companion, compass,
and advisor, of whom she asked, What
is the name of that bright red unseen bird?
This is East Prussia, perhaps, and the beaten
armies drag through the orchards leaving a trail
of dented canteens and coal scuttle helmets.
The soldiers walk right past her, they know
death when they see it: always the withered
flowers and haunted look of a girl
going nowhere and a road that stops
while seeming to go on. Always someone
lifting tea through its own steam
as he writes on a yellow pad.
Always the disgrace of his probing
and then the rain
dark as blackbirds falling into ditches
the girl would see if she could see anything
but rain. And what does the Kaiser have to say,
now? The soldiers are through listening
and after a while the tea is cold. The ragged child
picks a few flowers and asks their names.

2. A Tense Shift Addresses the Imagination

What did you want,
brass bands? April raining
crocuses and asters, crack
of the bat somewhere
and the crowd erupts?
Think of the year it snowed
all spring and whatever
you needed became its own
tattered ration
that would neither bloom
nor set a broken candle by the door.

Old lost soldiers stained
the yellow lamplight then, and salt
on the wrist of the angel of salt
prayed she be taken up out
of her shame.
What made her think of a father's
saying, "No, I don't remember. It was
wars ago. We fought
and covered the ground
like snow that one year, in April,
before you thought
or were born."
Sun will rise and green buds
burst like silent shellfire
and the old world roll
on its back again, ready

to love what is left. A name,
deep in the stems, hunkers, out
of ammo and starved for time.
Footprints lead away
toward a girl's voice carved
like a cross
in the deep sky of a tree.
Under the hungry snow and mud, imagine
millions of these.

3. Goodbye to All That

for Robert Graves

Down the lane from Highgate
thinking of tea, the Burmese red leaf
which we imagined only
the most magnificent pashas
could drink before sundown rang the call
to evening prayer. We were a trail of roses
and didn't speak.
We could have been anyone, a haunting
inside us all the way to Platform C
where we shouldered our weapons
still thinking of tea
and embarked, six hundred of us,
like a single song a rose might sing to scissors.

Women were there to see us off
and did. Well, ta-ta, we said. Off to feed
the cowardly Hun his liver.
Home by Christmas, so we said
and climbed aboard
and went off toward the sea.
It was a long way to Tipperary, it was
a long way to go. More women
smiled and waved us up the gangways
and our colonel gave a speech.
For Old England, he said.
Pro patria, he said. The brave die but once,
etc., and we laughed like dogs,

thinking of tea and the beautiful slow
meadows edged with green
and the little mill with its brickwork
and our fathers saying, Son, keep low.

And then we disembarked in Hell
and Reece went to pieces from the shells
and men fell like grain before the scythe
and we wrote home that all was well

and the Emperor joined our encampment
in the far north of Gaul
and we fought to the last man
at the Greasy Grass and burned the ships
and the cities
singing like heroes drunk with blood
joyous and despairing in the Teutoburg wood
with its piles and piles of skulls.

And at teatime we wept
and when we came home we were dead
and walking up toward Highgate with nothing
but dead flags in our arms.

4. I Thought

of the dead pilot, Manningham,
deciding not to be German
anymore, how the lily would be his flower
and rain his substantive arrest under the blossoming
lindens in, maybe, Stockholm, after the war.
I thought of men turned to blind, deaf afterthought
in the lead mines where air refuses its own dull blue
face, its shaking hands and knees gone to smashed crystal.
I thought of old men singing like crows in that pub
down under the bridge in Kraków, how they wept
and laughed and sighed and counted their change
and cracked their tight-mouthed smiles and went away.
I thought there must have been something lost
or monstrous in my heart, with its jangling ring
of keys, its ribbons darkened by prayer and women
who shivered and left or came back to touch
the little wooden horse inside my chest, turning its head
to see which path was glowing and where, finally,
the river of my better nature lay
like a surprise, and where my boat spun and drifted
leaflike and mortal toward the falls loud as traffic
or gunfire or applause. And I thought of the sea, also,
dark and bright and brimming
and my old shirt and shoes in that morning
when I wear them as my mind walks into the distance
toward Stockholm
to await the next war, or another helping
of the one that never ends.

5. War of the Worlds

The creatures from beyond Andromeda
arrive at noon
in little egg-shaped tubs of pink water.
Their blue eyes are also hands
grasping everything in a wink.
Their mouths are sky-sized presumptions
containing all the dictionaries in all the tongues
of all the worlds drifting forever
toward "God" or "Oblivion," the mysterious
final words it is their theology to regard
as a single possibility.

The national debt, the new improved Buick,
same-sex marriage, strength of the yen against
the dollar: these, and much else, wake in them

a singular dearth of fascination. In fact,
they've barely noticed us, their minds
having splashed on toward a teleology
beyond all substance but the sun.
They love the sun, its perfect placement
and moderation, its heat in which
they evaporate, condense, and are born
falling, soaking us all, sweeping like breath
over the lakes and streets and gardens
where we muse or toil at making the world
that is already here.

Each night the clouds and straight, wet streets
enact their perfect form. "All things exist
because they do," the alien sages say.
But we've had enough.
We call out
the National Guard and make them pay.

6. Saint Second Amendment

He shot the children first
so they wouldn't have to see him
shoot the parents.
He didn't care about the parents, they were
an absence already
in their dirty little two-bedroom hovels
with chickens in the yard
if they were lucky and had a yard.

The screaming was bad but didn't last.
The blood was bad, so he moved on
to the next house where a man attacked him
with a hoe.
Short work there.
And the children, the woman, walls, and sky,
he made them all
die with his swift, high caliber praise. Clearly

it was meet and right to do this. Even reloading
was like prayer. And surely some of them did
pray, and surely he answered beyond
happiness, cruelty or reason
until his power stood above them
perfectly alone.
Death is godliness, he thought, and I have come, legal
as time, to give you all its precision and display.

7. In This Photograph Baron von Richthofen

is standing with another pilot
at the aerodrome outside Cappy.
His cocky knifelike smile and handsome face,
hat tilted back, suggest a happiness
beyond fear and far
beyond regret for the eighty Allied pilots
he has sent down in shrieking flames.

Away over the Channel in England
his cousin, Frieda, has fallen
in love with D. H. Lawrence
for whom the Baron represents
the Thanatos of sexual power, the "flying"
and the "guns" a dead giveaway.
But soon, as he climbs into the cockpit,
he will review his three cardinal rules:

> 1. When hunting, stay up where others are
>   unwilling to go.
> 2. On the attack, come down out of the sun
>   like a bright surprise.
> 3. Never fly near the ground except to land
>   or strafe.

Because he will violate this crucial
third rule, it is the Red Baron's last day on
or above the earth. Shot through the chest
by ground fire, he will crash-land

his Fokker triplane in a field of wild asparagus
and all England (minus the Lawrences) will rejoice:
"Got the bugger at last!"—though he will be buried
by the RAF with full military honors.

But as he sweeps down over the field
he will be anticipating two weeks' leave,
the beautiful Marlina firmly
in his sights as he rolls and dives, imagining, perhaps,
Lawrence looking up from a steamy sentence
that has almost reached a climactic
though basic truth.

In this photograph, his insolence is so perfectly contained,
he cannot have heard Death say, You *are* handsome,
and so proud, I've been thinking of you and
of all you've done for me, and now
I'd like to do something
for you.

8. Meltdown

It was all somehow accounted for
in the ledgers of those who served

the kings and commissars of an orderly
distribution and control

that everything was theirs, even the crushed
knuckles of the stones, even the stiff

facsimiles of our brethren who had vanished
before us into that green flash

above the sundown sea. The whales, the dodo,
the great apes, all irrelevant as beauty, disappeared

like beauty, leaving only their names scratched
next to our own in the halls of unopening books.

We might have prayed for God
to come, or Noah, and deliver us

two by two again, drowning our terrible machines.
Now the oceans rise to take us

all. The stars go out. The angels, weary of extinctions,
shake their heads. But what were we to do, force

the powerful to change?

9. The Angel of Mars: Two Views

I.

I am unmoored, drifting like this

coppery cloud above the flattened cities.
The long parade of raggedness, unhinged
dustiness of roads
down which the troops have passed
like violent cursing and barns on fire
are what I am
and also bloated bodies and the whores
offering anything, everything
for bread or a magical leftover chunk of ice.

Shoot me.

I am history's torn out
page with which the vacant child
wipes himself. I disintegrate in stink and rain
that burns against all logic
like an argument between bricks
someone was, at last, too tired to carry.
I am duly elected king of that tiredness
and I vote to impeach myselves, among whom I confer
endlessly
as a preventative,

and I don't listen.

So it is, almost by accident, I uproot
the garden of well-being. Every day I am this
accident, plugging its ears
and turning to stopped clocks
for guidance. So it is I have learned nothing
from the past
and detest the past. I am the future
built by silent acclamation and its rotten flowers.
I am the gift no one will live to see.

II.

He said he was red because of so much
bright darkening
in the branches and, of course, because of the enemy.
He said he followed them
into tunnels and found them in the trees
like birds. Also they were like vines
or tigers, he said, their shadowed bellies blue
with the cold of fear and brave deception.
He said his watch stopped on a lost dime
and called home, listening for time's execution
like the boy with no feet or a man
whose face blew off while the rest of him danced
into a black plastic bag. He said, turned out that girl
he loved was dead-letter smoke in the rain
of a ringless bell, a wedding bell
it seemed. He said because of the rain's coolness
and the way it forgot everything, the general rouge of being
hardly troubled him. He found skulls, in fact, their gleaming
redness, when fresh, particularly soothing. We didn't
like the way he looked at us. But he said
to step back, allow room, and we would see much of him
become a mist of snakes and birds and jungle hours
framed by the principle of continuous reloading, that he was
our creature and that there was little left of him now
but what we and the fallen red angel of Mars
refused to know.

SCOUT'S HONOR

During the Oregon Centennial
celebration, my Boy Scout troop, dressed
as cowboy cavalry, was brought to the dog track
to rout a whole tribe of Cub Scouts
dressed as Indians
in a wild reenactment of a battle
that had never occurred
or had occurred a thousand times, depending

on your degree of historical specificity.

Firing our cap pistols and screaming for blood
we surged down
upon the menacing village of pup tents and "Indians,"
who ran, throwing down their toy spears and arrows,
in genuine terror.

The crowd in the grandstand cheered,
even when we began clubbing and trampling
those who were too small or slow
to escape through the gate to the parking lot,
even when one child, blinded by his tears,
ran headlong into a post and did not get up,

even when we pretended to take scalps.

Afterward, our scoutmaster herded us quickly
onto the bus, looking over his shoulder
with a crazed and worried smile.

It had been a perfect reenactment
and, in the true spirit of scouting, a lesson: this is what you do
to enemies, no matter how small or hapless or outgunned,
no matter whose stupid idea, no matter who dies
or who remembers it for the rest of his life.

REFLECTION UPON PSALM 121

I will lift up mine eyes unto the hills.
I think of that line
again as blossoms blow with rain.
Beyond the orchard
someone sings. Birds cant their heads
to ask if this is the tree they remember, if the refugee
finds refuge, truly.
Steam rises off the pond; or is it
a cordite fog, the numberless dead floating like lilies
in its breath. And if I do lift up mine eyes,
what beauteous face, what refuge from disaster,
what old beloved place?
God is a tree on the moon
inside us. And of its fruit
shall we not eat? Our loneliness, beyond all hunger,
says we must.
This is the refuge toward which all
the frightened and expelled move with breathless
care, as if they might spill themselves.
How perilous
then to lift up one's eyes.

ANCHORS AWEIGH

1. Tag

We were in the Arctic
playfully chasing a Soviet submarine
that was just as playfully tempting us, an endless
undeclared game of hide-seek-chase and
Oops! *There* you are! The boys in the Combat
Information Center having a wonderful time
for days, until the quarry slipped gigglingly
under the ice
leaving us shuffling and crestfallen as children
after the neighbor boy has scooped up his ball
and gone home. But there we were

above the seventy-fifth parallel in June, calm
seas and the sun never going down
as we cruised the edge of the ice pack, hoping
the Russian would come back out and play.

Sun upon the face of the practically
glassy deep. Once in a while an arctic tern
or albatross hovered to see what we might be.
Here and there a bit of drift ice, blinding
blue white.

We carried five thousand men and enough
firepower to destroy half of Asia, every inch
of the 41,000 ton ship absolutely dedicated
to this potential.

I stood on the hangar deck looking out
past the number-three elevator at the gemlike
expanse of sunlit 1:00 a.m. and found it almost
hard to credit hate or fear enough to turn us
into what we surely were.

Then the call to general quarters, like
someone banging on an iron pan in a phone booth.
Our friend was making a mad run for Murmansk.
The admiral was happy again.
We launched our choppers and put all eight
boilers on the line.

2. Religious Experience

Once during a lightning storm at sea
a man danced on the flight deck
and loosed a sort of singing
in a language no one knew.
The MAA's men stood around, confused
and blustering, "Look at that dumb fuck!"
to hide their fear. The lightning
brought his image in jagged,
cinematic flashes
so that at times he appeared to walk
the black air like a demon, like bad news
that was almost there.

And we were, ourselves, such news, an ark
of grey menace, choppers and fighters lined up
two by two and a red glow from the depths
in which we lived, "trampling out the vintage."

The man, Boatswain's Mate Second Class Pendarvis,
danced and danced
until the Captain said, "That's it, get the son of a bitch
down to sick bay," and they hauled him off, legs flailing, voice
a leaping imprecatory psalm, lightning blasts separating
one moment from the next
as we were, in fact, separate each from what we thought
the world should be.

But Pendarvis danced on, even in sick bay, singing
in Sumerian or Mu, and the chaplain,

having been sent for, arrived
frowning and helpless as a man of peace on a warship,
which is what he was.

3. *Limes*

I have been thinking of limes
and Lisbon, the narrow steepness
of the stair-step streets where old
black-clad women sat in doorways
with the fruit spread before them
like emeralds or pieces of the sea.
I bought one to chew and suck on
as I walked, passing through sudden
and secret plazas, mobs of children
shocked still by the strange
blue extravagance of my uniform
and my undeniable foreignness.

When I sat on a bench to
rest and enjoy the bronze image
of José Travassos Valdez, a hero
on horseback, water jetting
from his upraised sword, they crowded
to me like a flock of worshippers,
their huge eyes insisting here at last
was the time of miracles returned.

Having no candy and no Portuguese,
I drew in my notepad a picture
of the ship that had borne me there,
which they touched
as though it were the handiwork
of an angel
and begged for more.

I was there for hours, drawing
my city, house, car, family, the Statue
of Liberty, Mount Rushmore, the golden
arches of McDonald's, every scene
or shrine I could remember.
But what they loved best was a poor
depiction of my grandfather's orchard
and the man himself in it, bent among
his trees. This they passed around
and round, finally handing it back
with solemn genuflections to the gnawed
remnant of that lime I had not
shared with them
and had been too busy to throw away.

4. *Night Watch*

Since I was late relieving him, the man
on midwatch shook me
awake and I knocked him flat
on his ass. Just a reflex, I said,
helping him up, staunching the blood
with my T-shirt. Sorry.
Topside it was black-hair dark
but for starlight and the ember-like glow
of the binnacle. Look
slightly to the side of any movement, they said,
with the iris
not the pupil. So I stood at my station massaging
my stung knuckles, dreaming a little
with the ship's pitch and roll.
Three points and a hundred yards off the starboard bow
a great shape rose and went down
into the dark cities of shells and salt
where accident and malice made a homeland
for the dead. And there we were
skimming above it like insects, looking askance
at every danger, sign, or visitation, fists
ready for war
and the silence afterward.

5. Lifeboat Dream

We whiled away the war, coffee cups welded to our fingers,
our determination to survive shining like headlamps

as we moved between decks or topside among the wind
and spray.
        And surely delusion loved us, though we didn't care.
The enemy was far away, the music of his semiautomatic
faith like a squall on a distant island or a party in a convent
for the blind.

Darabaris was busy faking *somnambula majora*, bucking
for an early out.
        Louis Columbo ran a little loan operation
from his desk in disbursing: easy terms—at first.
        And my old friend Lavell kept losing
his clothes in quick exits from women's apartments, torching
his life at both ends and the middle. Once, exhausted by the mad
pace of his life ashore, he went down
on a woman and fell asleep, head on her fragrant belly.
Hey Lavell, we said, where'd you get the shiner? And
what happened to your pants?

        Lieutenant JG Tufts, younger
than any of us, whom we called "Sonny" behind his back,
was tall and smacked his skull on the overhead
every time he stood up.
        Johnson, quietly
and with enormous pride, did no work whatever.

A St. Elmo's fire of sea light, stack gas, and rage danced
in our hair and made us conditional, rented,

victims of an actuality deficit to be paid, somehow,
by smoking hash in the Legal Office or teasing the marines

or throwing "inessential" equipment overboard.
Sometimes I would dream of a huge green door

I had to open. Night after night, all my strength bent
to the task, I believed success might bring

a knowledge so exact I would escape the shipwreck
of that time and wander on home as though

unchanged. When at last I jimmied the door
ajar, there was the great diamond blue

sea and all of us in a rubber boat, bristling like a clutch
of baby owls, confused by wind, water, and the moon,

charting the course assigned us, our stubby oars flailing
and threatening to break.

6. If the Moon Kept Goats: A Veteran's Tale

I can't believe I'm saying this
again after so many years, but those things that keep
coming back
name us
and we have to let them in.

There was a war.

Unquenchable roaring bells surrounded it
like a woman on fire inside a dress. Some of us
were taken away on ships to be part of this
and came back full of broken furniture, our faces
black kites over a field of ice.
We had walked in harm so wrong and deep,
not even the sandman would let us sleep.

And me? I was a case.

I left everything lie like dead thieves in a bank,
and, beyond loyalty and war, set my desperate bones
to hold a woman
who could barely hold herself
inside the world become a world
I didn't know.
And what if she had left her husband then
and the light by which we thought we knew ourselves
had not failed, as it does, when we needed it
exactly?

What if the moon kept goats?

As I touched her to lure happiness out
of its tormented cage,
I thought of my father's faithfulness
and wondered how it was,

and by what right, he had returned from his
war and fashioned
from the remnants a whole
life.

I thought of the Southern Cross and the enemy—then
now and always—looking up, as we had,
but breathing easy, minds luffing a bit, buoyed out
by the wonder of clarified commitment
and it occurred to me that from a certain point of view
there was no hope at all.

I saw things in the trees.
I stopped eating salt
and grew a red shadow which drifts with me
still under the April wood, circling
a candle of dead confusion, unable to blow it out.

Think of that.

Think of a whole generation of us, hands
in our fathers' hands
and the sun seething with impossible conjunctions, war
on both sides of us and love
in between.

THE SITUATION

They were there and we were where
we were, each side waiting for the other to dig in
or declare. Tomorrow we would tear the body's veil,
as would they. Maybe tonight we would invade their sleep
or they ours, advance scouts having crept up on the pickets
and cut their throats in that special, noiseless way they teach you.
Maybe we would slip away before dawn, a cloud of dreams suddenly
remembering its nature. But who could tell? Some place and time
would ring with blows and burning men run mad with that red
you cannot live without. Anyway, there we all were, so close
in the dark we could smell each other's fear, its soft bark
bribing hope with the faces of those we loved. Time
refused whatever we wanted it to do, each second
becoming a half second and then an hour, a life.
We oiled our weapons and kissed the charms
hidden pathetically just above our hearts.
Then it was dawn. Bright sky and the
mourning dove calling in its tree.
Here they come, we thought.
Or here we come. Or,
once again, here
we all are.

TWO ENDINGS

I.

Will it be the house
burned black and kinked as a creature
struck by lightning? Might it be bags of tangled fingers
and mold, a wind full of hammers
and half-chewed razor blades in which we will be
forced to roll, the only gods there laughing
so hard their eyeballs bleed? It couldn't be
so bad the roads forget
to go on and a ditch swallows Mozart
again. Of course
it will have to end in the beautiful
morning of no one
stepping from God's mangle into the empty fields
of praise. The shadow of a thimble
quaking at the edge of a stream.
Bits of hair and bone.

II.

Tell me again I wanted a new hat
with a string you tighten under the chin.
A horse, certainly, also,
neck bent down to the grass, maybe
a watch with a blue crystal.
Dusty road, surely, and the hazelnut trees

pretending to sway.
A few tools in boxes by the bicycle.
Jars on a shelf. A dog
to follow me up the path.

3.

THE UNATTAINABLE NOW

The passing away of people and things is not the only secret of time.

Which calls us to overcome the temptation of our serfdom.

And to put on the very edge of the abyss a table,

And on the table, a glass, a pitcher, and two apples,

So that they magnify the unattainable Now.

—CZESŁAW MIŁOSZ

TWO BIRDS

Did you find the city of isolated men beyond mountains?
Or have you been holding the end of a frayed rope
For a thousand years?
—JAMES WRIGHT

The frayed rope swings with breeze,
nothing on the end of it
except the mind, perhaps, or my father
sharpening his saw in the side yard,
the last bit of orchard spreading arthritically
above him. Up there, too, a sky
of purple and sand blue clouds
masses like thought, though my father
thinks only that he needs a better file,
that it will rain in thirty-five minutes,
that he is dead and indifferent to this.
He probably knows how hard it is
not to touch his arm or whisper
his name
just above the shying of the breeze, the mild
screech as metal complains to metal
like two birds pulling at a worm.
Now and then he pauses and looks
at my form almost beginning to appear.
How *long* it takes, the work of being,
standing on one foot and another
as I do, handing him tools and asking "why"
six times a minute, playing absently

with the dog. And there is so much
to do, my father's beautiful face, its calm
attentiveness, tells me
as he straightens to view the sky again, certain
it will rain in a thousand years, that we will enter
that house gone to strangers and rubble
and lose ourselves, each of us reaching out
for what we must have been together
long ago and tomorrow and after the rain.

THE LIMITS OF MERCY

It was Tough Tony Borne strutting
in the ring again, having thrown
Gorgeous George over the turnbuckle
into the third row and a great clattering
roar of smashed folding chairs.
Beside me on the couch my grandmother
shook her head and made a disapproving
sound with her lips.
Tough Tony beat his chest.

As his vanquished foe struggled to climb
back through the ropes, he took hold
of that cascade of broom-colored hair,
lifted, like the Citizen holding up King Louis's
head beside the guillotine, and gave George's
face a well-placed knee. "Oh!"
my grandmother said. "Mercy." Then
we reached into the blue bowl between us
for more popcorn.

MY YOUTH

I'm still holding a girl's hand
by a fence in the dark schoolyard
after the dance class our parents insisted we attend.
Her blue dress still grazes my knuckle as we move,
dreamy and embarrassed, springtime softening
the little light there is, or would ever be.

I still believe if I touched her light
brown hair, I would be transformed, ennobled
by its lustre
as Arthur was ennobled when Guinevere turned
that first time and looked
straight into his eyes, the total clarity of that.

I'm still slipping out as the house dissolves in sleep
to walk through rain past the doomed berry farms
and empty fields. At the slouching Grange Hall, the one
caretaker is drunk again, and, as I pass, holds up his arms,
a little like Moses, that the waters part and spare us all.

He's still there, surely, if, walking backward, I could
undo the knots of cold disaster, the freight train
of unremarkable days with their immense load
of nothing I could name.
I'm still in canoes, baseball games, fistfights
and drive-in movies with their huge, godlike screens
and sputtering speakers. Still tasting
my grandmother's raspberry pie. Still stealing my first
slugs of whiskey and getting too smashed to stand.

Next day I'll be singing in the choir beside my father's
booming baritone, and thinking of that girl again,
the one who comes back in her blue dress
always, who holds my hand
without speaking, who danced with me all through
those years of tedious lessons, who looks
straight into my eyes.

HE SPEAKS TO THE MUSE

Don't tell me
you heard your name again, falling
from the mirror behind you,
stroking a little groove in the dust.
It couldn't be that
called you back
to sit by my window full of rain.

What do you want
with me now, old love
who couldn't find her shoes,
who made herself a rose of empty sleeves
mourning their arms?
Tell me again how far I've walked
without you, that I've forgotten your shape
beside me
all those years
forgiving the smoke of their destruction.

Veil of grey thread, tell me what you can.
Rain is your mother and your face
striking dead matches where marsh birds fluff
and huddle from the cold.
I count you on my fingers and still
there is only one of you
missing, and one of me here,
feeling the cool air part
as though a window had passed through me
and left itself open.

THE NOTHING THAT IS

For the listener, who listens in the snow,
And, nothing himself, beholds
Nothing that is not there and the nothing that is.
—WALLACE STEVENS

1. Ghosts

They are like doors you suspect
behind you, or something extra dark
in a corner of the darkness
when you're up late by a window
wondering how much time each
moment might contain, or if
your hands aren't more like wings
in denial.
Tinnitus may be their language, a kind
of laughter-laced ringing, the sea's
voice in a shell: every time you listen
there it is, so
close, a freezing thin
longing in every grey room of a house
deep in what you might imagine
is that ancient wood where the giant
wanders his giant sadness
and the wicked witch weeps for children
who will never bother her again.
Where when you open the door
there's a wall or an empty field
listening hard, as though it knew you.

2. *Author, Author*

The snow came circling
down like the midnight white-clad woman
dancing with her dog as I stood
dreaming of her beautiful arms, the half-shell
alabaster of them tuliped above her
as she stepped and turned and the dog
ran, circling, mad happiness itself,

and Pirandello sat back in his chair.
It must be so. The woman and the moon's dog
snowing.

What was I doing there, fast

asleep, covered with lumber while a bell
hooted and flew from my treelike fingers?
Pirandello is thinking of it still
in his stony house outside Palermo.

So much solitary dancing. A life
of secrets from which we cannot wake
no matter the hour or moon
or depth of snow. No matter how lovely
her arms.

Is that all? Are you one
of the Six Characters, *up all night*
in your empty clothes?

Yes, that's all. There would be no howling
and the snow came down
and she danced
and there was no author. Even the lunatic, his wife
nailed into her house and he bound
to a stone post in the courtyard,
knew that.

3. Your Brother's Face

You believe your brother will come down
after the rains
and sit rocking with you through the twilight suicides
of moths against the bulb
that hangs from the ceiling like an answer
or a bald old man on fire with love.

He will be tired, your brother. Wearing tired moons
on his fingernails, he will tell you the train that brought him
ran on shadows, the fireman feeding them into a vat
of black flame as the stars emerged and an owl
flew among them, looking for whatever secret thing
might hide and breathe and never make it home.

He will say it is better to forget
than forgive and show you a photograph of a blind man
waving to an empty field. How long has he been
standing by that hill where the road stops?
Surely in town the bars have closed their faces
and your brother's face turns toward you, more beautiful

than young, like something tarnished
but glimmering. If it's a stranger's face, you're home
and your brother is all around you under the lamp.

4. A Man in the Park

"It was beautiful
beautiful." There was nothing more
he could tell me
about life, he said. Wear a clean shirt
I think he mentioned
the Psalms and the mystery of a dog's loyal fascination.
He gave his wife a whole sentence and a half
before turning to swimming pools and fresh
baked bread. It was beautiful, beautiful
and I was all he had
to bear witness and applaud how this was so
right to the end! he said, where you feed
the pigeons and see sun break
the black lace of winter branches, where you call
one more time, silently, for a glimpse of the cream
and pearl sweetness of women languorous and desiring and turn
to the man beside you on the bench and say, "Beautiful.
Beautiful."
I was suffering my youth, sitting still
at a hundred miles an hour (did I have *time* for this?).
Even so, I couldn't help listening. His voice and the smile
inside it were the park itself, something
fractured out of a lovely and diabolical machine.
The sun went down. I let him go on for years and years
and years. It was beautiful.

5. Masefield in Purgatory

Falls and stays flemished,
lifts and braces squared,
we came in on the neap
under a single scrap of sail.
How long had we been out
and where, the wharfinger
did not ask. He could see
the answer far out behind us,
anyway, following on a shadow
or a piece of ancient spar
looking for home.

Contentment walked away
uphill from the sea and left us
bumping gently at the darkening
pier. If we announced ourselves,
who left us or appeared?
If we slept, what women touched
or woke
our beaten contemplations?
Beautiful beautiful return, sky-sized,
angelic and looking the other way,
kept its own council. Fair wind
was beside the point.

Still, as night came on, we laid
our offering of shells and string
on the grey planks, and prayed

that death relent and bless us,
who had come so far.
And the stars, as always, lit
their little fires in that dark
above the crisp sweet air.

6. Second Message

She sang, or I thought that
she did.

"My Melancholy Baby," "Stardust"
hung in the slightly blue air

by a white and broken
concertina

against which children stood
measuring themselves.

All night? Did this go on
as we slept?

She was like cream
over a bowl of cherries

set in a window beside the King's
mistress. Is that who

she was, aching before us,
counting beads with an

ivory pin? When we came
fully awake, she lay

next to us
a moment. Hummingbirds,

gash-like at their throats,
hovered over her

like a message not quite
forgotten and not quite known.

7. Abide with Me

I woke and checked to see
that she was breathing
then went to brush my teeth and stare
into the mirror.
Was it my face there
after all?

When I returned to her bedside
my mother had left herself like a scrap
of song risen into that dark
corner above the drapes, that niche
she could never quite get at
with the broom.

Pale orb up there
waiting for dawn, she was indifferent
to all grief and peril
and to my face grown suddenly young
in the presence of that mysterious kindness
every day of her life had insisted

we remember.
Then light filled the room.

IS TIME THE ROAD OR WHAT
TRAVELS ALONG IT?

My dog disappeared on a Friday and my parents said, well
it was one of those things.
They wouldn't look at me.

The girl who cried in the sixth-grade cloakroom
every morning so that the teacher shook her and said, "Shape up!"
disappeared as well,

like the meanings of things, *veritates rerum*: the Iceman's knife
and spoon, for instance, waiting five thousand years
for their next meal.

The farm, they said, finally. We took him
to the farm.

A beautiful place, I imagined, as everyone
who has ever lived has imagined a changeless meadow
near the sea.

And what of the sea, another sort of road, Beowulf's
whale road, St. Brendan's miracle passage. Now Neptune
rises in a robe of PCBs and medical junk, ice
slides away from the polar pack
like great chunks of cocaine.

Are we shaping up yet? Is that girl at the farm, too?

How will the traveler know
he has arrived

if all destinations turn to paths?

For years I thought of the farm, my dog romping
in the endless sunlit grass. Though I knew what the truth
must have been, I simply believed otherwise.

This is how the traveler arrives.

A WILLOW LIFE

Down the long Egyptian hallway
of the second grade
at Binnsmead School I said hello
to some of me and goodbye to the rest
as the dust relaxed and snow
hid in the future's darkened cloakroom
where Howard Grohs
showed me his satanic-looking stuffed iguana.

That was lifetimes back, before the wars
of women
and the war itself.
Before the three-headed pleasure of flying
out of one life into a seething undiscovered
coast of flailing statuary and targets
taunting their arrows,

where I said hello to a box of watches
out of time, that had come down to me
through time, their stillness a perfection
which may be experienced
but not remembered, since memory is revision
which perfection needs not.
And this is related to my refusal
to bow before the drownings that have cursed my family
with consecutive rain-like disaster
for four generations.

At last I said hello to the ancient sycamores
on 24th Avenue, their huge silence
a swatch of roses in the mind, the street itself
beautiful with birds and children. It made sense
to praise them
though I felt unworthy, though I had abandoned
so much

and so many I hardly understood what praise
might mean. I said hello to death.
I said I'm sorry. I said let me live
awhile by the untroubled
water unashamed and swaying, new leaves
all down my arms.

FALLING

You fall in love
and the sparrows fly back
to their small trees like a god
in fragments.

What to do then?

In the sky something circles
like a lesson on the laws of flight,
the ghost of Baron von Richthofen
in his Fokker triplane, looping
in a blaze of gunfire,
his enemies falling
in love
and deadly precision, an ecstasy
of grey sunlight.
I remember the moments
of sudden descent, the softening
features of the face in a room
or a car or a park with swans
enacting ourselves exactly
like death's dissolution of time,
the ailerons on fire at last,
the osprey plunging, the dull boy
in the spelling bee inexplicably
remembering "Zambezi,"
all those years in the back row,
drawing circles and lightning bolts

while the class strode off
over the hills, canceled in midair,
swept up into the body's truth
on fire. It happened
only a few times, each one
the first and last mission, all fear
cast aside, small bird singing
in the hawk's dominion.

THE BODY AT REST

No one was in the cellar
but she lit a candle and left it there
so dark might savor its definition
and its spirits warm their hands.
She had no hope at all
that truth would wake and climb the stair
blinking its mirrorlike eyes, refusing
all remorse and singing in the ancient tongue
of spiders who are never lost.
She knew the candle would burn out
and nothing be the same
old nothing she had known.
She knew rain would strike the window
like tiny birds ignorant of glass and time, perfect
having flown and fallen, having done
exactly what they are.
She was calm.
She stood still near a door
completely.

BIOGRAPHY

When they tore down the barn
they found bits of tack and harness,
sleeping messages from the kingdoms
of dirt and rust, the shadows of ancient horses
smoking out of them like sadness
and blowing away.

When they dozed up ground where the barn
had been, they found the grave
of a '27 Ford pickup
surgically altered to serve as a poor excuse
for a tractor.

They chopped down the orchard, dug
out the berry rows, flattened the greenhouse,
installed a paved lane and then a row
of double-wide rentals.

When at last nothing remained
of the old place but the pit from which
they had extracted the Ford, they planted a few petunias
around it, imagined it might make a fine
fishpond, went away
and forgot it.

Others came and built and stayed
and went away.
Rain continued in its season. Wind

uttered its choral remarks. The cloudy light
seemed to love nothing
but black branches and grass, once in a while
a bright red leaf.

TAKE ME OUT TO THE BALL GAME

for Scott Farnsworth

I lay on my back on the strip of lawn
between our house and the Eklands',
listening to the ball game as the narrow sky
darkened, waking the first stars.
The moon was low and big, the home team
winning. George Freese was up
and you could hear the crowd's expectancy and
praise, like leaves stirring in the summer branches.

A huge moth circled in the light from my bedroom
window, as though it had something to tell me.
Freese smacked a double off the wall,
clearing the bases, and my small radio filled
with a surf-like surge of celebration.

Everyone I loved was with me still, even my dog
and the sleek and philosophical black cat, Fang.
The grass beneath me was cool and soft.
I thought how it must be like this
for the angels: nothing to be
but what they were. God lolling on his back
somewhere, happy to be among them, almost
absentmindedly switching on the rest of the stars.

IN THE HOUSE OF THE AFTERLIFE

I woke in hiding, the cellar door dim
as an old man rising from his knees
in a storm. Nevertheless I found my way
to the kitchen's yellow robe edged with blue
forget-me-nots and saw my father musing
about birds as he rowed away
in a marvelous wooden bowl.

Others were smiling with the joy that thrives
past exhaustion and beyond
each river with its boatmen, joking about death,
and white goats wandering among ruins
along the shore. The newborn king
of windows poured with light
into which I stepped
and was changed.

Now on the top floor, open to the sky,
something made of music is ablaze
and God whittles angels, one for each poor
soul among us. Our days are spent
on the burning wheel of instruction, teaching them
to say, "God be with you." And them teaching us
to hear it.

MEMORY'S DAYBOOK

I.

Each night my mother tucked me in and said,
"Tomorrow is a new day," and each day the
gold and green orchard rose from a black glove
spattered with the paint of stars, proving her
right as peaches in a porcelain bowl, right as the
soft face of the breeze that followed me up the
path to the barn where my grandfather stood,
admiring his tractor.

> Blue heart of the peach pit
> hums
> and holds its breath
> like a candle.
> Love is its own soil
> and shoes. Sometimes
> the dog barked
> for joy.

II.

When the top thirty feet of a Douglas fir fell
on the house, my grandfather shook his head,
climbed the tree's remaining thirty feet, and
sawed off the splintered top, leaving a kind
of nest of upwelling boughs encircling the
flattened trunk. For years, when no one was
watching, I would ascend to that soft enclosure
and lie, looking up into the blue. Such dreams
I had! Such endlessness there, where no one
would ever find me.

> Light wanted itself
> high up, refreshed, clean
> in the resinous boughs.
> Alone, I was a single
> grey-bird-like boy
> swaying, a bit of green
> pencil
> in my pocket.

III.

She moved among the trees and the bars of sun, gathering apples into her apron and telling me stories of the old days in east county when there were blizzards and droughts and bears. Bending and smiling, occasionally showing me the ruby brilliance of a particular windfall and shaking her head with pity as she pointed out the bruises, she seemed like an orchard spirit, loving its bounty, rescuing the bright globes from sure shameful destruction on the compost heap behind the greenhouse. I stumbled behind her, loading my skinny arms with dented gravensteins and dreaming of pies.

> If we are lucky
> there is a time when
> so much is made evident
> by love
> we hardly need to know
> anything else.
> Look! On the bright face
> of the apple,
> a mourning cloak
> butterfly!

VOICE

for Madeline DeFrees

The last horse on the place
was Ronnie, blind, lame and sweetly slow
as a memory in which you lean back
looking at the sky.

He could still plow
between the berry rows, but had to go home
for lunch
and then for sleep beside the '32 Oldsmobile
in the grey, flat-roofed barn.

In my dreams he is huge and bright
as Heaven, high-stepping down Stark Street,
called Baseline then, bearing me, straight and proud,
through Russellville, the village that is no more.

He is not spavined, knock-kneed, and ragged,
not dead for more than sixty years.
Sometimes before sleep, or after, I feel
his muzzle soft against my face.
And someone calls to me
out of the dark.

A LAST WALK IN THE QUABBIN

for Galway Kinnell

We went down the path between birches
and white pine, stone walls
running off among them
into the abandoned fields.
Woodpeckers beat larval delicacies
from blighted chestnut
trees lying in their hundreds like dead soldiers
on a hill.
Water blazed in the distance.
The clarinet crying of loons met us
to suggest the strangeness of the actual, its perfect
lastness which is like friendship
in the way one aches because of it
and we wondered if we were really there, if our shadows

could hear us or if they had somehow their own lives
and did not care.

You had decided our thoughts
were not what we were saying, that intention
was far behind us
showing its blank cards to a dreamer
who would laugh about it later and send obscure congratulations
to the wrong address.
Beside a tumbled foundation
we found an ancient well, lifted the capstone
and tasted the sweet, dark water

that had been listening
for our shadows in a stillness like that
of the world itself
when at last we are through with it
or it through with us.

LOVE'S LAST NUMBER

for Emma, in memoriam

She was four years old when she told me
the children at her daycare had been arguing
over which was greater, infinity (pronounced
"finity") or the last number.

Sometimes we're speechless because we deserve to be.
Sometimes love leaps out beyond enumeration
or the vast, starry spaces in the skull of time.

With a secret, satisfied smile, she said, almost to herself,
"Jeremy says it's the last number, but we really know
it's finity."

And now she has gone like a sprite
into the genius of her answer, leaping every number, sailing
into the endlessness of that smile, and left us
plodding knee-deep in starless equations
in which X equals loss, again and again
and again, to the nth power.

Jesus said our days are numbered.
Hermes Trismegistus said numbers were the secret words
by which the world and heavens told each other
what would ever be.

And now we say a thing that matters
"counts."
And when it stops counting it is dross.

We say to measure is to know
and to know is to possess. But love
burns without consuming and weighs nothing,

like faith,
like a fool's precision or the dream of a memory
of a child's face.

The seventy-two names of God, the ten thousand things, too,
are nothing
to the one indivisible life, the sweet and singular falling
plum
and the spirit that flies away.

STEP BY STEP

I was hitchhiking once
through northern Ohio, rain all down the miles
betwixt Toledo and Sandusky where I stood
like a blurred photograph
in the backwash of the semis. I remember a momentary
vision of heaven, blue shells bordering a daisy field.
But night was coming on and the headlights began
to seem murderous. At full dark

I crossed the road to a pasture and slogged into a quiet
spinney of summer trees.

It can be beautiful to be alone when you are young
and indifferent to death.
I sat down against a huge oak and slept.

Snarling monsters with blaring eyes rushed toward me,
turning to water as they passed.
Something in the treetops wondered *who*.
I kept sinking and rising toward the woman I was
on my way to see.

No one knew me then, even the Devil had a hard time
placing me. In my sleep I wondered if an angel
had worked its way into my bones, I felt so light.

Then the moon came out red
over a field of stainless steel corn. I saw something ride
across the high clouds. I hugged myself hard

and wept, but it was not the woman I wept for, it was the wonder
of time's completion, that perfect freedom
of the lost.

At dawn I woke. I had twenty-six dollars, one for each
of my years on earth. To hell with women.
I would get breakfast, somewhere, and go north
into the UP, maybe

Ontario, and work in a boatyard.
I would buy a new shirt and become one of those
nameless men
distrusted by grocers and landlords, hoarding a secret
not even they themselves could understand. Both memory
and metaphor would forget the life I was leaving
there in the field
and it would become the field.

I shouldered my pack, and step by step
brought myself here.

WYOMING

I walk out into the hour
of the morning star
just as the birds begin.
Below me the river says itself.
In a dark field beyond the road
a light comes on and another
goes out.

There is no God
or there is,
leaning on a fence somewhere,

waiting for dawn.
He lifts a steaming mug of coffee,
adjusts his hat
and becomes a woman
or sleep or a tuft of grass.
What but absence
isn't God, I think.

ACKNOWLEDGMENTS

Some of the poems in this volume have been previously published as indicated below. The author wishes to express his thanks to the editors responsible.

Basalt: "The Parable as Originally Told"
Bellingham Review: "Meltdown"
Beloit Poetry Journal: "Edvard Munch"
Cascadia: "Two Poems in Which He Thinks of Her," "Lifeboat Dream"
Cerese Press: "Diminishing Returns"
Cloudbank: "Take Me out to the Ball Game," "In this Photograph Baron von Richthofen"
Copper Nickel: "Religious Experience"
Crazyhorse: "Edward Hopper," "Tiny Bees Clung to Us"
Field: "Ghosts," "Desperately Composed," "War of the Worlds," "Second Message," "Author, Author"
Gettysburg Review: "Limes," "My Youth," "Two Birds," "An As-Though Prayer," "Connectivity," "Goodbye to All That," "Love's Last Number," "A Short Song," "The Situation," "But before That," "Astronomy Lesson"
Glassworks: "Step by Step"
Hubbub: "Memory's Daybook," "Tin Soldiers"
Image: "Reflection upon Psalm 121," "I Said to God, 'I'm Thinking of You,'" "Scout's Honor"
The Journal: "A Man in the Park," "Falling," "Two Endings"
Louisville Review: "Kansas"

Massachusetts Review: "Wyoming"

Miramar: "The Limits of Mercy," "Voice," "A Tense Shift
    Addresses the Imagination," "Is Time the Road or What
    Travels along It?"

Plume: "Your Brother's Face," "Masefield in Purgatory"

Poetry Northwest: "On the Nature of Things," "The Body at Rest"

Prairie Schooner: "If the Moon Kept Goats: A Veteran's Tale"

Redactions: "He Speaks to the Muse," "The Angel of Mars: Two Views"

Rock & Sling: "Abide with Me," "In the House of the Afterlife"

Smartish Pace: "Saving Face"

South Dakota Review: "Crossing Jordan," "I'm Not Sure about Dying"

Sou'wester: "The Body in Motion"

Terrain: "Biography," "A Last Walk in the Quabbin"

"Crossing Jordan" appeared in *Naming the Unnameable*, ed.
Michelle Bonczek Evory (Binghamton, NY: SUNY Press, 2016);
and on the *Poetry Daily* website, January 3, 2015.

"Lifeboat Dream" appeared in *Best of the Net 2013* (Sundress
Publications).

"Tiny Bees Clung to Us" appeared on the *Poetry Daily* website,
July 13, 2011.

I would like to thank the Washington Artist Trust, Eastern Washington University's Committee for Research and Creativity, and the Ucross Foundation for the support that allowed me the time and psychological space necessary to complete many of the poems in this book. I wish to thank also Lex Runciman, Melissa Kwasny, and David Axelrod for their generous and helpful commentary, and for their steadfast friendship as well.

Joni Sternbach

Born in Portland, Oregon, Christopher Howell is author of eleven collections of poems, including *Gaze* and *Dreamless and Possible: Poems New and Selected*. He has received the Washington State Governor's Award, the Washington State Book Award, two National Endowment Fellowships, two fellowships from the Washington Artist Trust, and the Vachel Lindsay and Helen Bullis Prizes. His work has made three appearances in the Pushcart Prize anthology, and may be found in many journals and anthologies. A military journalist during the Vietnam War, since 1975 he has been director and principal editor for Lynx House Press and is now also director for Willow Springs Books. He lives in Spokane, where he is on the Master of Fine Arts faculty of Eastern Washington University's Inland Northwest Center for Writers.

milkweed
editions

Founded as a nonprofit organization in 1980, Milkweed
Editions is an independent publisher. Our mission is to
identify, nurture and publish transformative literature,
and build an engaged community around it.

WWW.MILKWEED.ORG

Interior design by Mayfly Design, and typeset in Arno Pro, which was created by Robert Slimbach at Adobe. The name refers to the river that runs through Florence, Italy.